A Chocolate Bar

W

FRANKLIN WATTS

LONDON • SYDNEY

This edition 2009

Franklin Watts
338 Euston Road
London NW1 3BH

Franklin Watts Australia
Level 17/207 Kent Street
Sydney, NSW 2000

Copyright © Franklin Watts 2005

ISBN: 978 0 7496 8961 2
Dewey classification number: 664.5

Series editor: Sarah Peutrill
Art director: Jonathan Hair
Design: Jemima Lumley

The Publisher and Author thank The Day Chocolate
Company for their help with this book.

A CIP catalogue record for this book is available from the
British Library.

Printed in Malaysia

Franklin Watts is a division of Hachette Children's Books, an
Hachette UK company.
www.hachette.co.uk

Photo credits: AKG Images: 17c. Cadburys/News Team International: 21,
23c, 27bl, 27cr. The Day Chocolate Company: front cover cl, 1l, 5b, 7tr, 8,
19bl, 25t, 26tl, 26cl, 26bl, 27br. Fiona Duale/Divine Chocolate: front cover tl,
b, back cover t, 1r, 4t, 11b. Geri Engberd/Image Works/Topham: 24t. Mary
Evans Picture Library: 15b, 23b, 24b, 29. Owen Franken/Corbis: 20t, 27c.
Ron Giling/Still Pictures: 15t. Masterfoods: 11t, 22b, 27tr. Richard
Melloul/Sygma/Corbis: 18, 27tl. Ray Moller/Franklin Watts: 28. Brian
Moody: front cover c, 6b, 7bl, 7tl, 9tl, 10bl, 12t, 12b, 26tr. Museo de America,
Madrid/Dagli Orti/Art Archive: 9br. Museum of London/HIP/Topham:
20b. Kim Naylor: front cover cr, 14tr, 16t, 16b, 23tl, 25b, 26cr, 26br. Christine
Osborne/Ecoscene: 4c. Karen Robinson: back cover c, 6t, 10tr, 13t. Karen
Robinson/Panos: 31. Georgia Glynn-Smith/ABPL: 17t, 19tr, 27cl. Sven
Torfinn/Panos: 14bl. Mireille Vautier/Art Archive: 13b. Peter Wilson/Holt
Studios: 5t. Every attempt has been made to clear copyright. Should there
be any inadvertent omission please apply to the publisher for rectification.

Contents

Chocolate is made from cocoa beans.

▲ This milk chocolate bar contains cocoa, milk, sugar and vanilla.

Follow the story to see how the beans become a chocolate bar like this one. The story starts in Ghana, West Africa, where the beans grow inside pods on cacao trees.

▲ Cocoa beans grow inside a pod.

The beans are taken to Europe. In the Netherlands and then Germany they are made into chocolate.

► Most of the chocolate eaten in the UK is made from cocoa beans grown in Ghana. American chocolate bars are also made from cocoa grown in West Africa, as well as cocoa from Central and South America.

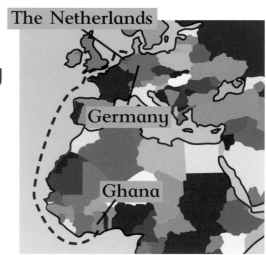

The Netherlands

Germany

Ghana

First the farmer prepares some land in the shade of some trees. He plants cacao seeds and the trees begin to grow. Cacao trees are often planted in rainforests or under banana or rubber trees.

Most cacao trees in Ghana grow on small family farms. Three to five years after planting the seeds, the trees burst into flower.

Cocoa pods develop from these flowers.

▲ Each tree produces about 10,000 tiny flowers, from which about 20 to 30 develop into cocoa pods.

▲ The cocoa beans inside the pods are the seeds of the cacao tree.

Where do cacao trees grow?

Cacao trees only grow near the Equator where the weather is always hot and wet. They originally grew in the rainforests of South America. Seeds were taken from there and planted in equatorial Africa, the Caribbean, Malaysia, Sri Lanka and Indonesia.

When the pods are ripe, the farmers cut them down.

Every year each tree produces between 20 to 30 pods, containing about 40 beans per pod. The pods turn yellow or orange when they are ripe. The green ones are left on the tree.

The farmer is careful not to harm the pods or the tree as he slices the ripe pods off.

▲ The farmer uses a sharp blade, or machete, to cut the pods off the tree.

The whole village joins in with the harvest, which happens twice a year.

◄ This woman is carrying harvested pods to a collection point.

Now the farmers cut the pods open.

▲ A close look inside a cocoa pod.

Inside there are damp white cocoa beans resting in pulp.

▲ The farmer splits the pods open with a sharp blade.

The pulp and the beans are carefully scraped out of the pods into baskets. At this point the cocoa beans taste very bitter. The pulp, however, tastes sweet.

◄ The pulp and the beans are kept together for the time being.

The pulp and the beans are piled onto leaves.

The farmers use dark green plantain leaves for this job. Plantains are a type of banana tree that often grow alongside cacao trees.

The farmers wrap the leaves around each heap of pulp and beans to create leaf parcels.

The parcels are left in the sun for between five and eight days.

◀ A heap of slimy beans and pulp.

Inside the leaf parcels it becomes really hot. The heat makes the pulp ferment, which means that bacteria and yeasts in the pulp multiply. This releases chemicals that change the flavour of the beans.

The pulp turns to liquid and drains out of the leaf parcels. The beans are taken out of the parcels.

In the past

The Maya people lived in Central America, just south of where Mexico is today, from the 4th century CE. They are the first people to have left records of making a drink from cocoa beans. The Maya roasted, pounded and fermented the beans with maize and pepper. They called the beans *cacao* meaning, 'food of the gods'.

The Aztecs (see page 13) learned to make a chocolate drink from the Maya. They poured it from a height to make it frothy.

The farmers spread the beans on village drying tables.

It does not usually rain in Ghana at harvest time. This means that the beans can be left out in the open, on drying tables made from bamboo. The farmers take it in turns to turn the beans over.

➤ People turn the beans to help them dry, picking out any bad ones.

It takes between five and twelve days for the beans to dry.

◄ The beans are regularly checked for quality.

As the beans dry they shrink in size. Now they look very different from the damp white beans harvested from the pods two weeks earlier.

► The beans have shrunk because they have lost a lot of the water inside them.

What is Fairtrade chocolate?

This chocolate bar is made from fairly-traded cocoa beans. This means that the cocoa beans were grown under good working conditions. The farmers received a fair price for their cocoa beans and were sure of a buyer every time. Fairtrade farmers are not as poor as many cocoa farmers in the past, or in other parts of the world today. For more about Fairtrade, see page 30.

Fairtrade chocolate companies make many types of chocolate.

The dried beans are put into sacks.

▲► The sacks are filled and sewn up.

The beans are sorted so that the beans in each bag are the same quality. The farmer and his family have done everything so far, from planting the seeds to sewing up the bean sacks. Now they can sell the beans.

The farmer's sacks are checked for quality and weighed. This is done by a man called a recorder. He also arranges for lorries to collect the sacks.

For now the recorder pays the farmer half the value of each sack, making sure he pays a fair price. The recorder pays the farmer the other half after the sacks have been sold to Cocobod (see next page).

▲ The village recorder checks the weight of each sack and keeps careful records.

In the past

Today the price of cocoa beans can vary. The Aztecs, who settled in Central America from the 14th century, used the beans like we use money. Four cocoa beans could buy a pumpkin, 10 cocoa beans equalled a rabbit (to eat!) and 100 beans bought a slave.

Aztecs offer Hernadez Cortez (see page 17), an honoured visitor, their much-valued cocoa drink.

The cocoa beans go on a journey.

First the sacks of beans are loaded onto lorries.

➤ It takes two men to load each sack because they weigh 62 kilograms!

▼ Cargo ships can carry hundreds of sacks.

The full lorry is driven to the capital of Ghana, Accra. Here the government cocoa board, Cocobod, buys all the sacks of beans. As the farmers belong to a farmers' cooperative (see page 31), they get a better price for their cocoa beans than other farmers. Now the sacks are loaded onto cargo ships, which set sail for Europe.

The sacks of dry, hard cocoa beans arrive in the Netherlands for the next stage.

▲ Men pile up the sacks of cocoa beans once they arrive at the port in the Netherlands.

Why do the beans go to the Netherlands?

In 1828 a Dutchman named Conraad Van Houten invented a machine that could press 50% of the cocoa butter out of the beans to leave dry cocoa cakes and rich cocoa butter. Although some chocolate companies, especially in the USA, have built their own cocoa presses, much cocoa is still pressed in the Netherlands, or in Germany.

An early advert for Van Houten cocoa powder, 'The best of all the drinking chocolate'.

In the factory, the beans pass through many stages.

The workers split open the sacks and pour the beans into a sorting machine. This sorts out the different sizes of bean and cleans them.

► The factory workers often mix sacks of different types of cocoa bean to get a good-tasting chocolate mixture.

Then the beans are roasted at a high temperature to improve the flavour further and to kill any harmful micro-organisms.

◄ The beans are roasted for between 10 and 35 minutes at temperatures of 120°C or more.

Now the cocoa beans are so brittle that the next machines can break them open and blow away the shells with jets of air. This is called winnowing and it leaves just the cocoa nibs.

➤ The leftover bean shells are removed.

In the past

How did chocolate spread to Europe?

Christopher Columbus and Hernandez Cortez were European explorers working for Spain in the early 16th century.

Columbus bought back a few cocoa beans to Spain in 1502 but it was Cortez who saw the value of the cocoa bean. In 1528 he brought back a cargo of cocoa beans from Central America with the tools to make the chocolate drink. It became very popular in Spain and from there spread to the rest of Europe.

When Columbus landed on Guanaja, Central America, in 1502, Aztecs brought him gifts including a sack of cocoa beans.

Rollers grind the cocoa nibs into a liquid.

This brown liquid is called cocoa liquor and it has a very strong chocolate flavour. The liquor flows off the machine into shallow containers.

Some of the cocoa liquor leaves the factory at this point to go to the chocolate factory. The rest goes through another stage.

Cocoa liquor contains a fat called cocoa butter. This butter is squeezed out of the leftover cocoa liquor using a powerful machine.

▲ Rollers squash the nibs and turn them into a brown liquid.

What is left is solid cakes of cocoa powder called presscakes, and cocoa butter. The cocoa butter is used to help make chocolate, as well as soap and skin creams.

The presscakes are ground down into a powder. This is then sold as cocoa for hot drinks, or used to flavour cakes, biscuits or ice cream.

▲ Trays of finely ground cocoa powder wait to be put into tins.

▲ It takes up to a year's crop of cocoa beans from one tree to make one tin of cocoa powder.

In the past

How did chocolate get its name?

When the Spanish arrived in Central America (see page 17), where Mexico is today, they met the Aztecs. The Aztecs offered the Spanish a drink made from cocoa beans that they called *chocol haa*, meaning 'hot drink'. South of the Aztecs, the Maya used the word *chokola'j*, which meant 'to drink chocolate together'. Back in Europe people called the drink *chocolat* and then finally chocolate.

The liquor is loaded into tankers.

The cocoa tankers set off for the chocolate factory in Germany. Now the final stage of the chocolate production begins. The cocoa butter is added to the cocoa liquor. The extra cocoa butter makes the chocolate softer and more 'melt in the mouth'.

▲ Cocoa butter is poured into the cocoa liquor.

A scene inside a chocolate house in 1787.

In the past

Drinking hot chocolate was a popular pastime for rich people in 17th century European cities. Some people drank it at home but there were also chocolate houses. These were like clubs where men and women could chat or do business. At the time poor people could not afford hot chocolate. In the 19th century the price of powdered cocoa came down and then everyone could enjoy hot chocolate.

Sugar, vanilla and powdered or evaporated milk are also added at this stage. Now all the ingredients are mixed together.

The whole mixture is put through another series of rollers to mix everything up and make it really smooth.

Next the conching begins. This is when the chocolate mixture is stirred constantly at a warm temperature for a day or more. Gradually the chocolate develops an incredibly smooth texture and an even better flavour.

▲ All the ingredients of the chocolate bar are mixed in a huge machine.

The warm chocolate mixture is tempered.

The mixture flows into tempering kettles. These are large metal containers. In the tempering kettles, paddles keep the chocolate moving as it is carefully warmed and cooled.

▼ This chocolate has become very shiny and smooth after tempering.

The factory workers take great care as the chocolate could be ruined at this stage. Finally, when they are sure that the chocolate is ready, they push a button to let it flow into moulds.

◄ The factory worker tests the chocolate to see if it is ready.

In the past

The first true chocolate bar was made in England by J S Fry in 1847. He added some cocoa butter to a mixture of cocoa powder and sugar to make a chocolate bar. At first, only the rich could afford such a treat as it was expensive.

An advert for Fry's chocolate from 1907.

▼ The chocolate runs into the mould.

The chocolate is now cooled in its moulds. When it is cold the bars are tipped out onto a conveyor belt.

The chocolate bar is checked.

The factory worker checks the bars of chocolate, to make sure they are all good enough to sell.

◀ As the conveyor belt passes before her eyes, the factory worker looks for poor quality chocolate bars.

Is chocolate good for you?

Chocolate can be good for you as long as you don't eat too much! It is high in fat and sugar so it could make you put on weight. However, scientists have discovered that chocolate, especially dark chocolate, contains chemicals that can protect your heart against disease and help to prevent cancer.

In the past, chocolate companies were allowed to advertise chocolate as a healthy food.

CHOC-FULL OF GOODNESS!

Now machines wrap each bar in foil and put the paper wrapper on. Bars of chocolate are packed in boxes and then into lorries, which take them to shops in the UK to sell them. Some bars are also shipped abroad to countries such as the USA and Canada.

► It takes a whole crop of beans from just one tree to make between four and six bars of chocolate like this!

◄ The chocolate bars finally reach the shops. There are a huge range of chocolate bars to choose from. This is another Fairtrade chocolate bar.

How a Fairtrade chocolate bar is made

1. The cocoa pods grow on the cacao tree.

4. The farmers spread the beans out on drying tables.

2. The farmers harvest the ripe pods and split them open.

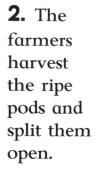

5. The beans are shipped to a cocoa processing factory in the Netherlands.

3. The pulp and beans are wrapped in leaf parcels and left to ferment.

6. Machines clean, roast and winnow the beans, leaving cocoa nibs.

7. The cocoa nibs are squashed to form cocoa liquor.

11. Next the chocolate is conched and then tempered, stirring all the time as it is warmed and cooled.

8. Some cocoa liquor goes through a press to extract cocoa butter, leaving cocoa powder.

12. The warm chocolate flows into moulds, where it is cooled and tipped out as bars.

9. In the German chocolate factory, the cocoa butter is added to the cocoa liquor.

10. Milk, sugar and cocoa butter are added to the mixture.

13. The bars are wrapped and packed, ready to eat.

More ways to use cocoa

How many ways have you eaten chocolate?

Chocolate shapes

Chocolate
muffin

Chocolate ice cream

Chocolate roll

Chocolate biscuits

Chocolate only uses the cocoa nibs at the centre of the cocoa bean.
Many other products use the rest of the cocoa pod.
Here are just a few:

➤ the husks of the pod are used to make animal feed. They
are also used to make soap and fertiliser
➤ the pulp juice is collected during fermentation and bottled
to be sold as drinks
➤ cocoa shells are used by gardeners to improve the soil
➤ cocoa butter is used in moisturising creams for the skin and
for soaps.

The original chocolate companies

Many of today's chocolate companies in England and the USA were set up by people who felt they should look after their workers. This was at a time when many working people suffered bad working conditions and poor housing.

△ The housing and environment of Bournville were much better than workers were used to.

New towns

In 1879 George Cadbury of the Cadbury chocolate company built a new factory, called Bournville, near Birmingham in the UK. He then built a village for his workers, including houses, shops and schools.

Other chocolate companies, like Rowntree and Terry's of York, also built houses, schools and training colleges.

In the USA, Milton Hershey built the factory town of Hershey in Pennsylvania. He then built a zoo and an amusement park for his workers' entertainment!

Fairtrade and Kuapa Kokoo

Fairtrade

You may have noticed the Fairtrade label on some of the food you eat. You can buy Fairtrade bananas, tea, rice, honey, coffee and many other products as well as chocolate. Most of these goods are grown in the poorer parts of the world.

Kuapa Kokoo

Kuapa Kokoo is the name for a group of Ghanaian cocoa farmers who have joined together to form a cooperative. It means 'good cocoa farmers' in Twi - the local language. Their motto is 'PaPa Paa' which means 'the best of the best'.

Fairtrade labels

The Fairtrade label means that:

➤ the farmers receive a fair, fixed price for their goods

➤ the cocoa buyers pay a 'social premium'. This means the community receives money for improvements such as healthcare and water

➤ the farmers have long-term contracts with the buyers of their goods

➤ the farmers work in good conditions and have a say in how the organisation runs.

Different countries have their own Fairtrade labels, e.g:

Guarantees a **better deal** for Third World Producers ® FAIRTRADE UK

USA and Canada

Look for this label on Fairtrade products

Find out more about Fairtrade at: www.fairtrade.org.uk

Working together

The cooperative works for the good of all its 45,000 members to help them grow and sell their cocoa beans. All the cocoa sold by Kuapa Kokoo is grown under Fairtrade conditions.

The Day Chocolate Company

Kuapa Kokoo owns one third of The Day Chocolate Company, which makes Dubble and Divine chocolate bars. Extra money made by the company is shared among the farmers who grew the cocoa in Ghana.

◀ Most cocoa farmers earn £125 per year in total.

The benefits of belonging to Kuapa Kokoo:
▶ the farmers earn more as a cooperative because they have better selling power and are more efficient at doing business
▶ at the end of the year, any profit made by the cooperative is divided up and paid as a bonus to each farmer
▶ Kuapa Kokoo pays for improvements to villages, such as better water supplies
▶ Kuapa Kokoo buys many tools at once, at a lower price, which they can sell on to their members
▶ Kuapa Kokoo organises training and education.

Word bank

Bacteria The name for many different types of very small single-celled living things that live everywhere.

Conching Part of the chocolate-making process. The conching machine stirs the warm mixture to develop a smooth flavour and texture.

Conveyor belt A constantly moving belt of rubber used in factories to move things about.

Cooperative A group of people who join together to work for a better life for them all, including better prices or better working conditions.

Ferment To make something bubble up or start to break down, often using yeast (see below).

Micro-organisms Tiny microscopic living things, some of which cause illness.

Tempering Part of the chocolate-making process. By constantly stirring, heating and cooling the chocolate mixture, it develops a shiny appearance and an even better flavour.

Yeast A group of tiny fungi that use sugar to grow. When yeast grows in cocoa leaf parcels, the pulp and beans ferment to develop the cocoa's flavour.

Index